0

Abraham Lincoln

in

Worcester;

AN ADDRESS DELIVERED BY

ARTHUR P. RUGG

BEFORE THE MEMBERS OF THE WORCESTER SOCIETY
OF ANTIQUITY
ON DECEMBER 2, 1909.

1914
BELISLE PRINTING AND PUBLISHING CO.
WORCESTER, MASS.

ABRAHAM LINCOLN IN WORCESTER

By Arthur P. Rugg

The figure of Abraham Lincoln in history has grown so commanding and this year's celebration of the centennary of his birth has been so widespread that any incident of his life arouses interest. Every locality which can claim a personal association with him acquires a new dignity. The places where he spoke, the scenes of his actions, the surroundings of even trivial events in his life, attract public attention. Therefore, it seems worth while to recall the circumstances of his visit to Worcester. He was here only once. That was in September, 1848, the year of the Taylor-Cass campaign. He was then serving his single term in the National House of representatives, to which he had been elected in the autumn of 1846, and, as at the age of thirty-nine he had declined a renomination, it must have seemed then that his participation in the affairs of government was likely to be brief and unimportant. In order to appreciate the significance of his visit to Massachusetts it will be helpful to consider briefly the political situation in the country. The presidential campaign of 1848 was unique in several aspects. Slavery was looming large above the horizon as a vital issue. The vote of the slaveholders was always in the eye of party managers. The Democratic party was wholly controlled at that time in the interest of the slavocracy. The Whig was the only party of national proportions, in which anti-slavery principles could hope to make their voice heard. The Whigs had been almost continuously a party of opposition since the beginning of

Jackson's administration in 1829, for the victory of 1840 had proved barren through the death of President Harrison within a month of his inauguration, and the sceptre of power had been wrenched from its hand by the political apostacy of Tyler. The annexation of Texas and the Mexican war had resulted in large additions to the territory of the United States, some of which was destined certainly for slavery, and a part of which might be won for freedom.

These events, fraught with momentous consequences to the future of our country and the weal of mankind, occasioned violent political discussions. The Whigs, although on other governmental policies reasonably united, comprised men of widest divergence of views respecting slavery. The satirical wit of Ebenezer Rockwood Hoar described the party as made up of "conscience" and "cotton" Whigs, the former regarding slavery as a moral issue, and the latter suffering their moral perceptions to be stifled by commercialism. The factions grew in strength and hostility until the meeting of the national convention in June, 1848. A powerful portion of the party proposed to make no declaration against the extension of slavery, and to select a candidate of such neutral principles as to be capable of representation as favorable to all views. The result was the nomination of Zachary Taylor, the military hero of the Mexican war, without any platform. Charles Allen, of Worcester, was a delegate to this convention. Aroused by what he regarded as the pusillanimous surrender of principle to expediency, he addressed the convention in a powerful speech, in the course of which he said: "The Whig party is here and this day dissolved. You have put one ounce too much on the strong back of northern endurance." He came to Worcester to become a candidate of the Free Soil party for Congress, and to justify his declaration of party dissolution by the irrefutable fact of achievement. Charles Hudson, of Westminster, had represented the district for four terms as a Whig. He was a Universalist minister. Although his

name now sounds strangely in our ears, he was a man of
distinction in the councils of his party. He was at this
time a member of the ways and means committee of the
national house, and a few months later was offered the
position of Secretary of Interior by President Taylor. . The
Worcester district was one of the important fields of that
political campaign. Charles Allen was no mean antagonist.
He was a foeman' worthy the most accomplished opponent.
The bolter from the national convention, who had declared
the Whig party dissolved, was a candidate for Congress
against one of the old and tried representatives of the
Whig party, who, although not a pro-slavery man, did not
sympathize with the radical views of the Massachusetts
Free-Soiler.

It was under these circumstances that Abraham Lincoln
came to Worcester. I have been unable to determine at
whose solicitation he made the trip to Massachusetts. The
late Hon. Edward L. Pierce, of Milton, in a letter* written
in 1891 to William H. Herndon, Lincoln's law partner and
biographer, says:

"I have wondered how Mr. Lincoln happened to come in 1848.
Mr. Winthrop, to whom I spoke on the subject, does not remember,
but thinks Mr. Charles Hudson, M. C., may have asked him. Mr.
Lincoln in Congress did not make much impression on Mr. Winthrop."

The suggestion, that he came on the invitation of Congressman Hudson, is supported by reasonable inferences.
Lincoln had acquired considerable reputation in Congress
as a ready and forceful speaker. His Massachusetts col-
league, older in the service, may well have recognized his
ability, and been won by his strength and attractive per-
sonality. . He was in Worcester on the night of the speech

---

*I am deeply indebted to Mr. Jesse W. Weik, of Greencastle,
Indiana, one of the authors of Herndon and Weik's "Life of
Lincoln," for the loan of this and other valuable letters.

by Lincoln, and himself addressed the convention on the
day following. Moreover, there appears to have been some
friendship between the two, for in 1861 Lincoln appointed
Hudson to the important and lucrative post of assessor of
internal revenue for the Middlesex district. Lincoln came
here on Tuesday, the twelfth of September, 1848, and
addressed a meeting held in old city hall on that evening.
In his eulogy before the city council and citizens of Worcester, on June 1, 1865, Alexander H. Bullock thus refers
to this visit:

"'At that time I met him in the streets of Worcester. Congress
had just adjourned when our Whig State Convention assembled
here in 1848. As the chosen head of the city committee of the
party with which he acted, I had called a public meeting in yonder
hall for the evening preceding the convention, and had invited
several gentlemen of note to make addresses. None of them came.
But as the sun was descending I was told that Abraham Lincoln,
member of Congress from Illinois, was stopping at one of the
hotels in town. I had heard of him before, and at once called
upon him and made known my wish that he would address the
meeting of the evening, to which he readily assented. I further
suggested to him that as the party in whose cause we were then
united was largely in the minority here, and as there was an un-
usual bitterness in the antagonistic politics of this community, he
should practice much discretion, and leave our side as well in its
prospects as he could. His benignant eye caught my meaning and
his gentle spirit responded approval. His address was one of the
best it had ever been my fortune to hear, and left not one root of
bitterness behind. Some of you will remember all this, but not so
distinctly as I do. The next day the convention came; the genius
eloquence of Choate, of blessed memory, was applauded to the
echo, and the stately rhetoric of Winthrop received its reward;
but the member from Illinois, though he remained in town sur-
rounded by associate Congressmen, was that day and in that body
unknown and unheard.''

Perhaps the inference from this narrative is that Lincoln
came to Worcester without a definite invitation to speak.
But the Whig State Convention of the day following, where
the party principles were expounded by Rufus Choate and
Robert C. Winthrop, whose reputation as orators and

statesmen was nation-wide, could not fail to attract a man like Lincoln.

Henry J. Gardner, Governor of the Commonwealth from 1855 to 1858, describes Lincoln's visit to Worcester in a letter which is printed in Herndon's Life of Lincoln, as follows:

"Gov. Levi Lincoln, the oldest living Ex-Governor of Massachusetts, resided in Worcester. He was a man of culture and wealth; lived in one of the finest houses in that town, and was a fine specimen of a gentleman of the old school. It was his custom to give a dinner party when any distinguished assemblage took place in Worcester, and to invite its prominent participants. He invited to dine, on this occasion, a company of gentlemen, among them myself, who was a delegate from Boston. The dining-room and table arrangements were superb, the dinner exquisite, the wines abundant, rare, and of the first quality.

"I well remember the jokes between Governor Lincoln and Abraham Lincoln as to their presumed relationship. At last the latter said: 'I *hope* we both belong, as the Scotch say, to the same clan; but I *know* one thing, and that is, that we are both good Whigs.'

"That evening there was held in Mechanics' Hall (an immense building) a mass-meeting of delegates and others, and Lincoln was announced to speak. No one there had ever heard him on the stump, and in fact knew anything abut him. When he was announced, his tall, angular, bent form, and his manifest awkwardness and low tone of voice, promised nothing interesting. But he soon warmed to his work. His style and manner of speaking were novelties in the East. He repeated anecdotes, told stories admirable in humor and in point, interspersed with bursts of true eloquence, which constantly brought down the house. His sarcasm of Cass, Van Buren and the Democratic party was inimitable, and whenever he attempted to stop, the shouts of 'Go on! go on!' were deafening. He probably spoke over an hour, but so great was the enthusiasm time could not be measured. It was doubtless one of the best efforts of his life. He spoke a day or two afterward in Faneuil Hall, with William H. Seward, but I did not hear him.

"In 1861 business called me to Washington, and I paid my respects to the President at the White House. He came forward smiling and with extended hand, saying: 'You and I are no strangers; we dined together at Governor Lincoln's in 1848.' When one remembers the increased burden on the President's mind at this trying time, the anxieties of the war, the army, the currency, and the rehabilitating the civil officers of the country, it seemed astonishing to me to hear him continue: 'Sit down. Yes, I had been chosen to Congress then from the wild West, and with hayseed in my hair I went to Massachusetts, the most cultured State in the Union, to take a few lessons in deportment. That was a grand dinner—a superb dinner; by far the finest I ever saw in my life. And the great men who were there too! Why, I can tell you just how they were arranged at table.' He began at one end, and mentioned the names in order, and, I verily believe, without the omission of a single one.''

The reference in this letter to Mechanics' Hall as the place where Lincoln spoke is of course an oversight, for he spoke in the old City Hall. Mechanics' Hall was not built until nine years later, having been dedicated on March 11, 1857.

I have made diligent effort to ascertain further details of the dinner given by Governor Levi Lincoln referred to in this letter. No doubt all who attended it have long since died. As was the custom in those days, the Whig convention of the following morning was opened by prayer, and Edward Everett Hale is reported in the newspapers to have made the invocation on that occasion. A letter from him under date of February 9, 1909, assures me that he had no memory of the occasion, and was sure that he never saw Mr. Lincoln in Worcester. The only further information I have been able to get about it is from another letter of Mr. Pierce to Mr. Herndon, dated February 12, 1890, in which he refers to a meeting held the Saturday before by the Massachusetts Club in commemoration of Lincoln's birthday, which was addressed by Governor Gardner, and after referring to the dinner at Governor Levi Lincoln's says:

"Governor Gardner gives names of other guests at table as Rufus Choate, George Ashman, George S. Hillard, Emory Washburn, A. H. Bullock, Charles L. Putnam and Stephen Salisbury. Of these Washburn and Bullock as well as Gardner were afterwards governors. I doubt if Governor Gardner at this date remembers names of persons at the table with certainty, and if Choate was present the dinner is more likely to have been on the

day of the convention than on the day before. Gardner repre-
sents Mr. Lincoln's address as most effective.''

Another report of Governor Gardner's remarks on the
same occasion credits him with having said, in referring to
the same dinner: ''The guest, also Lincoln by name, kept
very quiet.''

Mr. Charles M. Thayer of this city had a most interesting
conversation with Governor Gardner touching this dinner.
With his father, the late Judge Adin Thayer, he attended
as a lad a political festivity in Boston and was placed at
table beside Governor Gardner. The latter learning that his
young companion lived near the Governor Lincoln homestead, told the story of the entertainment there of the mar-
tyred President, saying that he sat opposite him as the
guests were arranged. Then he related the incident of his
visit to the President in Washington in 1861, and gave
these details in addition to those in letter quoted. President Lincoln said that he had always had a high apprecia-
tion of the culture and refinement of the people of Worcester; that the dinner at Governor Lincoln's by reason
of its elaborate hospitality and social brilliancy was dif-
ferent in kind from any function he had ever attended before. He remarked upon the beauty of the china, the fine-
ness of the silverware and the richness of all the table ap-
pointments, and spoke of the company of distinguished and
thoroughly educated men whom he met there in the ani-
mated, free and intimate conversation inspired by such an
accomplished host as Governor Lincoln.

The residence of Governor Lincoln at this time was
where his grandson, Mr. Waldo Lincoln, now resides, at
49 Elm street, but there is no tradition among the Worcester Lincolns of the dinner, which apparently made so
deep an impression upon the mind of the Western congressman. This, however, is not surprising, for his house-
hold was at the head of social life in Worcester for many
years, and his generous and refined hospitality attracted

to his board many persons, among whom were Lafayette, Webster, Clay, Adams, Everett, any one of whom at the time of his visit seemed far more distinguished than this congressman from the prairies.

The Worcester papers of the day give a scant report of the speech of Mr. Lincoln on this occasion. The Palladium merely mentions his name as a speaker. The National Ægis says of it:

"For sound, conclusive reasoning and ready wit it is unsurpassed in the campaign. It was listened to by the crowded audience with an untiring interest, applauded during its delivery, and enthusiastically cheered at its close."

The meeting was called to order by Hon. Ira M. Barton, president of the Rough and Ready Club. Ensign H. Kellogg, of Pittsfield, was chairman, and made a brief speech. The principal address was made by Mr. Lincoln. The Spy, then edited by John Milton Earle, an ardent Free-Soiler, was in its editorial policy violently opposed to the Whig party. A parade and speech of the following morning just preceding the state convention is described in the following language:

"At about 9 o'clock the Taylor Club to the number of some 50 or 60 preceded by the Worcester Brass Band proceeded from their headquarters to the Rail Road depot where they met a portion of the Boston delegates from whence they escorted them through one or two streets back to the depot whence the citizens numbering we should say some 700 to 800 were addressed by his Honor, the Judge of Probate of Worcester County, by his Honor, the Mayor of Worcester, by Mr. Taylor, senator from Granby,—almost a facsimile of old Zach. himself,—by a Mr. Woodman of Boston and by Mr. Abraham Lincoln, the recently defeated Taylor candidate in the 7th Illinois district in Illinois for reëlection to Congress. These gentlemen all said some good things that were rather witty, though truth and reason and argument were treated as out of the question, as unnecessary and not to be expected."

No reference is made to the meeting in the City Hall of the previous evening.

It will be noted that even this account is incorrect, in that it refers to Mr. Lincoln as "the recently defeated Taylor candidate in the 7th Illinois district in Illinois for reëlection to Congress." Referring to this two days later, the Spy says:

"The organ (referring to the True Whig) complains of our suggestion that Abraham Lincoln was a defeated candidate. We knew that a Cass man had been elected in his district, and hence inferred erroneously it appears that Mr. Lincoln was the defeated candidate. It turns out, however, that it was another Taylor candidate who was defeated, Mr. Lincoln foreseeing the danger having prudently withdrawn himself."

This was even more misleading than the first statement. Lincoln declined to be a candidate for reëlection because of a tacit understanding to that effect when elected.

The National Ægis in describing the out-door speaking of Wednesday morning, September 13th, which occurred on the balcony of the Foster street railroad station, then standing near the present Lowell block, at the corner of Norwich and Foster streets, mentions Lincoln among others as following Hon. B. F. Thomas "in short and happy speeches."

The most complete report of the speech is in the Boston Advertiser, and is appended to this paper. It is accompanied by this description:

"Mr. Lincoln has a very tall and thin figure, with an intellectual face, showing a searching mind, and a cool judgment. He spoke in a clear and cool and very eloquent manner for an hour and a half, carrying the audience with him in his able arguments and brilliant illustrations, only interrupted by warm and brilliant applause."

The Free-Soilers were much offended by a passage, which does not appear in the Whig reports. Referring to the antislavery men, he said they were better treated in Massachusetts than in the West, and turning to William S. Lincoln, of Worcester, on the platform, who had lived in Illi-

nois, he remarked that in that state they had recently
killed one of them. This allusion to the murder of Elijah
P. Lovejoy at Alton was thought by the Free-Soilers to be
heartless, and it was noticed that Mr. Lincoln did not re-
peat it in other speeches. It was probably a casual remark
which came into his mind at the moment, and found utter-
ance almost as an aside. It certainly could not have ex-
pressed any sympathy with the outrage.

With the aid of many friends, I have tried to find some-
one now alive who remembers Mr. Lincoln's appearance in
Worcester, but one person only has been found who has
any memory about it or who attended the meeting in the
City Hall. He is James Almon Fuller, now fourscore and
five. Not having kept a diary at the time, naturally his
memory is not very distinct respecting a political speaker
then and for ten years afterwards almost unknown in the
county at large. But he recalls the tall figure, plain appearance, and earnestness rather than eloquence of speech,
of him who was to be the great liberator of the slave and
preserver of the Union

Lincoln wore on this, as on a few other more signifi-
cant occasions, a long linen duster. He stopped at the
Worcester House. This was originally the Homestead of
Governor Levi Lincoln, erected by him in 1811, and occupied until 1834. It was then converted into a hotel, and
known as the Worcester House until about 1857 when,
the building known as the Lincoln House block having
been erected in front of it, the hotel was called the Lincoln
House, the name it still retains.

It is interesting to note the political associates and op-
ponents of Lincoln in Massachusetts upon this visit, and
compare their relative positions twelve years later, when
he was a candidate for the presidency. Winthrop and
Everett, on the same platform with him then, were hostile
to him in 1860, while Sumner, Wilson, Andrew and scores
of others, who opposed strongly his position in 1848, be-

came among his warmest supporters in the crucial contest
when the existence of free institutions was at stake.

As the Advertiser's report of Lincoln's speech in Worcester shows, he then thought that the solution of the slavery question lay within the Whig party. He regarded the
Free Soil movement as a sporadic ebullition of political
perversity, for he claimed that Free Soil was one of the
principles of the Whig party. Miss Tarbell, describing in
her "Life of Lincoln" his visit to Massachusetts, says that
he "won something in New England of vastly deeper im-
portance than a reputation for making popular campaign
speeches. Here for the first time he caught a glimpse of
the utter impossibility of ever reconciling the northern
conviction that slavery was evil and unendurable and the
southern claim that it was divine and necessary; and he
began here to realize that something must be done * * *
He experienced for the first time the full meaning of the
'free soil' sentiment as the new abolition sentiment was
called. * * * Sensitive as Lincoln was to every shade
of popular feeling and conviction, the sentiment in New
England stirred him as he had never been stirred before
on the question of slavery." It was toward the end of this
visit that he said to Mr. Seward, "We have got to deal
with this slavery question and got to give much more
attention to it hereafter than we have been doing." It
may well be that in this Heart of the Commonwealth, the
hot-bed of the Free Soil movement, whose delegate to the
National Whig Convention had declared the party dissolved because of its surrender to slavery, and which rati-
fied and rewarded his action by electing him to Congress,
and where, as declared by the inscription in the City Hall
composed by our great senator, was "organized the political movement begun to preserve to freedom the vast territory between the Mississippi and the Pacific and ended by
the abolition of slavery throughout the continent," he received an incentive toward the abolition of slavery, which

bore such glorious fruitage in the Emancipation Proclamation.

Lincoln spoke in Lowell, Cambridge, Chelsea, Dedham and Boston during this campaign of 1848, but never afterwards in Massachusetts. So far as I have been able to discover, none of these speeches were reported. Worcester has the distinction therefore of being the only place in the Commonwealth where a speech delivered by Lincoln has been reported.

SPEECH OF ABRAHAM LINCOLN

Delivered in the City Hall at Worcester on the Evening of September 12, 1848, As Reported in the Boston Daily Advertiser of September 14, 1848

Mr. Kellogg then introduced to the meeting the Hon. Abraham Lincoln, Whig member of Congress from Illinois, a representative of *Free Soil.*

Mr. Lincoln has a very tall and thin figure, with an intellectual face, showing a searching mind, and a cool judgment. He spoke in a clear and cool, and very eloquent manner, for an hour and a half, carrying the audience with him in his able arguments and brilliant illustrations— only interrupted by warm and frequent applause.

He began by expressing a real feeling of modesty in addressing an audience "this side of the mountains," a part of the country where, in the opinion of the people of his section, everybody was supposed to be instructed and wise. But he had devoted his attention to the question of the coming Presidential election, and was not unwilling to exchange with all whom he might meet the ideas to which he had arrived.

He then began to show the fallacy of some of the arguments against Gen. Taylor, making his chief theme the fashionable statement of all those who oppose him, ("the old Locofocos as well as the new") that he *has no principles,* and that the Whig party have abandoned their principles by adopting him as their candidate. He maintained that Gen. Taylor occupied a high and unexceptionable Whig ground, and took for his first instance and proof of this his statement in the Allison letter—with regard to

the Bank, Tariff, Rivers and Harbors, etc.—that the will
of the people should produce its own results, without Executive influence. The principle that the people should do
what—under the constitution—they please, is a Whig prin·
ciple. All that Gen. Taylor does is not only to consent,
but to appeal to the people to judge and act for them-
selves. And this was no new doctrine for Whigs. It was
the "platform" on which they had fought all their battles,
the resistance of Executive influence, and the principle of
enabling the people to frame the government according to
their will. Gen. Taylor consents to be the candidate, and
to assist the people to do what they think to be their duty,
and think to be best in their natural affairs, but because
he don't want to tell what we ought to do, he is accused of
having no principles. The Whigs here maintained for
years that neither the influence, the duress, or the prohibi-
tion of the Executive should control the legitimately ex-
pressed will of the people, and now that on that very
ground, Gen. Taylor says that he should use the power
given him by the people to do, to the best of his judgment,
the will of the people, he is accused of want of principle,
and of inconsistency in position.

Mr. Lincoln proceeded to examine the absurdity of an
attempt to make a platform or creed for a national party,
to *all* parts of which *all* must consent and agree, when it
was clearly the intention and the true philosophy of our
government, that in Congress all opinions and principles
should be represented, and that when the wisdom of all
had been compared and united, the will of the majority
should be carried out. On this ground he conceived (and
the audience seemed to go with him) that Gen. Taylor held
correct, sound republican principles.

Mr. Lincoln then passed to the subject of slavery in the
States, saying that the people of Illinois agreed entirely
with the people of Massachusetts on this subject, except
perhaps that they did not keep so constantly thinking
about it. All agreed that slavery was an evil, but that we
were not responsible for it and cannot affect it in States of
this Union where we do not live. But the question of the
extension of slavery to new territories of this country is a
part of our responsibility and care, and is under our control. In opposition to this Mr. Lincoln believed that the
self-named "Free Soil" party was far behind the Whigs.
Both parties opposed the extension. As he understood it,
the new party had no principle except this opposition. If

their platform held any other, it was in such a general way
that it was like the pair of pantaloons the Yankee peddler
offered for sale, ''large enough for any man, small enough
for any boy.'' They therefore had taken a position calculated to break down their single important declared
object. They were working for the election of either Gen.
Cass or Gen. Taylor.

The speaker then went on to show, clearly and eloquent-
ly, the danger of extension of slavery, likely to result from
the election of Gen. Cass. To unite with those who an-
nexed the new territory to prevent the extension of slavery
in that territory seemed to him to be in the highest degree
absurd and ridiculous. Suppose these gentlemen succeed
in electing Mr. Van Buren, they had no specific means to
prevent the extension of slavery to New Mexico and Cali-
fornia, and Gen. Taylor, he confidently believed, would not
encourage it, and would not prohibit its restriction. But
if Gen. Cass was elected, he felt certain that the plans of
farther extension of territory would be encouraged, and
those of the extension of slavery would meet no check.

The ''Free Soil'' men in claiming that name indirectly
attempted a deception, by implying that Whigs were *not*
Free Soil men. In declaring that they would ''do their
duty and leave the consequences to God,'' merely gave an
excuse for taking a course that they were not able to main-
tain by a fair and full argument. To make this declaration did not show what their duty was. If it did we
should have no use for judgment, we might as well be
made without intellect, and when divine or human law
does not clearly point out what is our duty, we have no
means of finding out what it is by using our most intelli-
gent judgment of the consequences. If there were divine
law, or human law for voting for Martin Van Buren, or if
a fair examination of the consequences and first reasoning
would show that voting for him would bring about the
ends they pretended to wish—then he would give up the
argument. But since there was no fixed law on the subject, and since the whole possible result of their action
would be an assistance in electing Gen. Cass, he must say
that they were behind the Whigs in their advocacy of the
freedom of the soil.

Mr. Lincoln proceeded to rally the Buffalo Convention
for forbearing to say anything—after all the previous dec-
larations of those members who were formerly Whigs—on
the subject of the Mexican war, because the Van Burens

had been known to have supported it. He declared that of all the parties asking the confidence of the country, this new one had *less* of principle than any other.

He wondered whether it was still the opinion of these Free Soil gentlemen, as declared in the "whereas" at Buffalo, that the Whig and Democratic parties were both entirely dissolved and absorbed into their own body. Had the *Vermont election* given them any light? They had calculated on making as great an impression in that State as in any part of the Union, and there their attempts had been wholly ineffectual. Their failure there was a greater success than they would find in any other part of the Union.

Mr. Lincoln went on to say that he honestly believed that all those who wished to keep up the character of the Union; who did not believe in enlarging our field, but in keeping our fences where they are and cultivating our present possession, making it a garden, improving the morals and education of the people; devoting the administration to this purpose; all real Whigs, friends of good, honest government,—the race was ours. He had opportunities of hearing from almost every part of the Union from reliable sources, and had not heard of a country in which we had not accessions from other parties. If the true Whigs come forward and join these new friends, they need not have a doubt. We had a candidate whose personal character and principles he had already described, whom he could eulogize if he would. Gen. Taylor had been constantly, perseveringly, quietly standing up, doing his duty, and asking no praise or reward for it. He was and must be just the man to whom the interests, principles and prosperity of the country might be safely intrusted. He had never failed in anything he had undertaken, altho' many of his duties had been considered almost impossible.

Mr. Lincoln then went into a terse tho' rapid review of the origin of the Mexican war, and the connection of the administration and of Gen. Taylor with it, from which he deduced a strong appeal to the Whigs present to do their duty in the support of Gen. Taylor, and closed with the warmest aspirations for and confidenec in a deserved success.

At the close of this truly masterly and convincing speech, the audience gave three enthusiastic cheers for Illinois, and three more cheers for the eloquent Whig member from that State.

Milton Keynes UK
Ingram Content Group UK Ltd.
UKHW021259231123
433136UK00019B/893